The Economics of Social Credit
and
Catholic Social Teaching

The Economics of Social Credit
and
Catholic Social Teaching

"Douglas's outlook followed
that evinced by Catholic tradition."[1]

The Economics of Social Credit
and
Catholic Social Teaching

© 2014
M. Oliver Heydorn

All rights reserved under international copyright conventions. No part of this publication may be reproduced, stored in a retrieval system, or transmitted in any form or by any means, electronic, mechanical, photocopying, or otherwise without prior written permission from the publisher.

ISBN-10: 1494946262
ISBN-13: 978-1494946265
Library of Congress Control Number: 2014902619
CreateSpace Independent Publishing Platform
Ancaster, Ontario, Canada

Contents

Preface vii

The Economics of Social Credit
and Catholic Social Teaching 1

Notes 59

Bibliography 73

Preface

There is, to be sure, much more that can and should be said concerning the relationship between Social Credit and the social doctrine of the Catholic Church than will be said in *The Economics of Social Credit and Catholic Social Teaching*. In lieu of an exhaustive exploration of the subject, the aim of the following text is more modest: it seeks to highlight some of the main points of commonality and contact that characterize the economic dimensions of Social Credit thought when viewed in light of the social teachings of the Church. As such, the information provided in this booklet presupposes a sound and relatively comprehensive understanding of both fields of study.

Those readers who are not very well acquainted with the thought of the founder of Social Credit, Major Clifford Hugh Douglas (1879-1952), and who are particularly unfamiliar with his economic ideas, may begin by reading the second, revised and enlarged edition of Bryan Monahan's relatively brief *An Introduction to Social Credit* (see bibliography). It would be best, however, to read this booklet immediately after or in conjunction with my recently published book, *Social Credit Economics* (available *via* amazon.com). The latter is a lengthy monograph specifically designed to provide an exclusive and more in-depth treatment of the economics of Social Credit for the more advanced and/or serious student. As far as Catholic social doctrine is concerned, readers who have no or an insufficient knowledge of the Church's teaching in this particular sphere should carefully examine the social encyclicals of the Popes (easily available on several sites on-line) and/or obtain a copy of the *Compendium of the Social Doctrine of the Church* (also freely available on-line).

The practical purpose of pointing out the extraordinary and comprehensive affinity which exists between the economics of

Social Credit and the Church's social teachings is to help Catholics to recognize the kairos and to respond accordingly. The financial and economic systems that presently govern the world are not only grossly unsatisfactory, their inherently dysfunctional character means that they are economically, politically, culturally, and environmentally unsustainable. That we are on the path to global disaster (and have been for a number of centuries) is becoming ever more apparent, even to the meanest intellects. Now, if Douglas' economic ideas correctly outline the type of solution which must eventually be implemented if equilibrium and well-being are to be restored to the financial and economic systems, and to the wider society as whole, individual Catholics and Catholic associations have been afforded a tremendous opportunity. On the one hand, the raw capacity of the various Catholic associations and institutions around the world to achieve intended results, what Douglas would have referred to as their 'social credit', is incalculable. On the other hand, in Social Credit, Catholics have been provided with a method, indeed the best possible method, by means of which the social teachings of the Church can be made flesh and the temporal order transformed in Christ. Consider what tremendous good could be accomplished if the social credit of the Catholic world could be harnessed, however unofficially, in the service of the Social Credit cause. While it would be beyond the scope of this little study to adequately substantiate, I am convinced that there is nothing on the natural plane that would do more to achieve the glorification of God, the exaltation and vindication of Holy Mother Church, the social reign of Christ the King, and the welfare (both temporal and eternal) of souls, than the intelligent and assiduous study and promotion of the theory and proper practice of Social Credit by the world's Catholic population.

Vive Christus Rex!

The Economics of Social Credit and Catholic Social Teaching

The reader may legitimately wonder why a whole booklet has been dedicated to exploring the relation that exists between the economic doctrines of Social Credit and the social teachings of a particular religion. The answer is simple: Catholicism bears a certain uniqueness amongst the various religions of the world where Social Credit is concerned. While it is not necessary to be a Catholic in order to be an advocate of Social Credit economics (grounded as it is in natural reason, Social Credit appeals to all men of good will), it is also true that any Catholic who is sincerely convinced of the technical case for a Social Credit economy should not only have no philosophical (or theological) objection whatsoever to Social Credit's remedial principles or its underlying social policy, he should actually be an enthusiastic supporter of a Social Credit economic reform precisely *because* of his Catholicism.[2] It seems doubtful whether such a pair of claims can be made at all or as strongly, *mutatis mutandis*, with respect to any other religious creed.[3]

In the first place, Catholics should have no philosophical or theological objection to Social Credit's general economic orientation simply because the social teachings of the Church are directly in line with the underlying social philosophy of Social Credit; nay, they are identical with that philosophy – a fact which should surprise no one as they ultimately derive from the same basic source.[4] This particular claim was, quite appropriately, reciprocally affirmed both by Douglas when discussing Social Credit's relationship to Catholicism and by a theological commission which was established by the bishops of Québec in the later part of the 1930's in order to pass judgement on Catholicism's relationship to Social Credit.

In the pages of *The Social Crediter*, Douglas clearly affirmed on a number of occasions that Social Credit was grounded in a Christian worldview and that the sociology of the Catholic Church was the purest expression of the fundamentals of that worldview as it related to social questions:

> We have from time to time expressed the opinion that the Roman Catholic outlook on economics and sociology is the essentially Christian outlook; and that no other Christian body of opinion is so consistent in its *official* attitude. It is beyond question that the anti-Christian venom of the Communists is focused on Roman Catholicism, and that Protestant bodies, when not used as tools (and even then), merely excite contempt.[5]

As far as the theological commission was concerned, their task was to undertake a general examination of Social Credit from the point of view of the Church's social doctrine and to determine in particular whether or not Social Credit partook of any of those various and numerous aspects of socialism and communism which had been condemned by the Church, and whether, in consequence, it could not be accepted or propagated by Catholics.[6] The nine theologians who composed the commission rendered the following judgement:

> To the question: 'Is Social Credit tainted with socialism?' the Commission responds, therefore, in the negative. The Commission cannot see how one could condemn in the name of the Church and of her social doctrine the essential principles of this system as previously presented.[7]
> [my translation]

In the second place, not only does Social Credit fully respect, in its theoretical framework, Catholic social principles, Catholics should also be enthusiastic supporters of Social Credit economics (if they are sincerely convinced of the technical claims, explanations, and arguments) because Douglas' remedial proposals represent a marvellous way of, and indeed, the best available set of methods for, concretely applying the Church's teaching in a manner that promises to yield consonant results. Just as 'faith without works is dead', the truth of the Church's social principles remain sterile if they are not incarnated in the real world through appropriate mechanisms. This is just one of the ways in which 'Social Credit is a necessity for Christianity.'[8] According to the teaching of the Church, it is above all the laity who have been entrusted with the task of conforming the secular world to the laws of the Gospel.[9]

Let it be made quite clear that this second claim is put forward on the basis of the present author's own judgement, and it is not, nor could it ever be, the official judgement of the Catholic Church. The Church does not possess the required authoritative competence (by her own admission) to render a binding judgement on the more technical aspects of an economic or political system.[10] Her social teaching is more or less *confined* to the level of broad principles. Accordingly, the Québécois theologians who examined Social Credit in the pre-Vatican II period explicitly and rightly refrained from passing any judgement on it whatsoever from a purely economic or political standpoint (which would concern Social Credit's technical feasibility, or whether or not it should or how it could be practically applied in any particular country). It is not the role of the Church to determine and then impose as doctrine those economic and political systems (etc.) which actually happen to work best in practice. All such matters are left to the laity and to other men of good will; people must seek to discover and to apply the objective truth for the greater benefit of mankind in these and all of the other fields of inquiry which happen to lie beyond the Church's legitimate jurisdiction as guardian of the deposit of faith. The most the Church can do in a strictly official capacity is to give a negative judgement, i.e., to condemn certain specific systems or certain aspects of them as unacceptable because they seriously violate, or portend to violate, one or more of the fundamental principles of the Church's social teaching.[11] This was the sort of test which had been administered by the Québécois theological commission and which Social Credit passed with flying colours.

At the same time, the freedom which the Church gives to the faithful to prefer a particular economic or political system over another *within the stated parameters* should not be misinterpreted, as some Catholics are wont to do, as implying that there is no right system which ought, objectively, to be supported *in conscience* by Catholics and indeed by all men of good will. The Church does not hold, nor has she ever claimed to possess, a monopoly on the totality of objective truth (there are innumerable truths and indeed many existentially important truths that lie outside of divine revelation). The fact, for example, that the Church has not given and indeed cannot give a wholehearted approval of Social Credit in any official capacity should not be interpreted by Catholics (or by anyone else for that matter) as a sign that in this case the truth does not exist, cannot be determined, is not important, or else that it ought not to be zealously promoted by a person possessing a morally awakened consciousness. Even though it is beyond the competency of the Church's Magisterium to evaluate the purely technical side of Social Credit economics or that of any other economic or political system, it is simultaneously true that 'Christianity is nothing without the incarnation'.[12] Certain extra-religious truths do indeed make serious, legitimate demands on people of faith.

The two basic claims that have been put forward in this introduction can be further brought to evidence by: a) engaging in a brief study of the essential content of the Church's social teaching in a side-by-side comparison with the social philosophy underlying Social Credit, and by: b) illustrating how the Social Credit reforms would allow 'the word to become flesh', i.e., how it would enable – finally – the Church's teaching to become integrally realizable in practice.[13]

As far as the social doctrine of the Catholic Church is concerned, the core of her infallible and unchanging teaching in this particular sphere can be reduced to four basic principles that ought to be respected by any and all human associations. According to the recently published *Compendium of the Social Doctrine of the Church*:

> *The permanent principles of the Church's social doctrine* [341] *constitute the very heart of Catholic social teaching.* These are the principles of: *the dignity of the human person* ... which is the foundation of all the other principles and content of the Church's social doctrine; [342] *the common good; subsidiarity;* and *solidarity*. These principles, the expression of the whole truth about man known by reason and faith, are born of "the encounter of the Gospel message and of its demands summarized in the supreme commandment of love of God and neighbour in justice with the problems emanating from the life of society". [343] ... *These are principles of a general and fundamental character, since they concern the reality of society in its entirety*: from close and immediate relationships to those mediated by politics, economics and law; from relationships among communities and groups to relations between peoples and nations. Because of their *permanence in time* and their *universality of meaning,*

the Church presents them as the primary and fundamental parameters of reference for interpreting and evaluating social phenomena, which is the necessary source for working out the criteria for the discernment and orientation of social interactions in every area.[14] *Compendium of the Social Doctrine of the Church*, nn. 160-161.

1. **The Primacy of the Human Person** – *"The sabbath was made for man, and not man for the sabbath."* (Mark 2:27)

The first principle of the Church's social teaching insists that the human person is metaphysically superior in comparison with any association; the individual and his legitimate interests are infinitely more important than the group. It is thus for the sake of the human person, his dignity and his authentic development, that the social world exists:

> **The permanent validity of the Catholic Church's social teaching admits of no doubt.**
>
> **This teaching rests on one basic principle: individual human beings are the foundation, the cause and the end of every social institution. That is necessarily so, for men are by nature social beings. This fact must be recognized, as also the fact that they are raised in the plan of Providence to an order of reality which is above nature.**
>
> **On this basic principle, which guarantees the sacred dignity of the individual, the Church constructs her social teaching. She has formulated, particularly over the past hundred years, and through the efforts of a very well informed body of priests and laymen, a social doctrine which points out with clarity the sure way to social recon-**

struction. The principles she gives are of universal application, for they take human nature into account, and the varying conditions in which man's life is lived. They also take into account the principal characteristics of contemporary society, and are thus acceptable to all.[15] *Mater et Magistra*, nn. 218-220.

C.H. Douglas also championed the primacy of the human person in social life. In his very first book, *Economic Democracy*, he wrote:

> Systems were made for men, and not men for systems, and the interest of man which is self-development, is above all systems, whether theological, political or economic.[16]

Indeed, by seeking to ensure that economic association will always operate in the service of the human individual to the greatest possible extent, Social Credit has made this arch principle of the Church's social teaching its leitmotif. Accordingly, the various financial reforms that Douglas proposed are designed to thoroughly subordinate the economic sphere to the well-being of the human person, in sharp contradistinction to the status quo, which, to a greater or lesser extent, subordinates the common individual to the needs and demands of the economic system. The correct identification of the true purpose of economic association in conjunction with the employment of the correct financial methods necessary to facilitate its adequate fulfillment promise to result in the liberation of the individual from the illegitimate domination of the group in economic matters.

2. **The Common Good** – *"Thou shalt love thy neighbour as thyself."* (Matthew 22:39)

The second principle of the Church's teaching is that social life, i.e., activity in association, only embodies an integral respect for the primacy of the human person when it is correctly ordered to something called 'the common good'. The common good, in turn, has been formally defined as "the sum of those conditions of social life which allow social groups and their individual members relatively thorough and ready access to their own fulfillment...."[17] Materially speaking, the Catholic understanding of the common good entails those policy-objectives which stand at the intersection between what legitimately lies in the general interest of an individual and what legitimately lies in the general interest of every other member of an association. In the words of Pope Paul VI, all associations must seek to "promote the good of every man and of the whole man."[18] This means that Catholicism conceives of the common good in a distributistic and not in a collectivistic manner, in terms of a real or concrete mutual advantage rather than an abstract aggregate good. It is the facilitation of the flourishing of each and every individual and not the fulfillment of the theoretical whole, or of some groups or individuals at the illegitimate expense of others, which must be the aim of every association.

Douglas likewise accepted mutual advantage as the normative goal of associations. As proof of this affirmation, consider his statement that Social Credit would seek to establish: "a society based on the unfettered freedom of the individual to co-operate in a state of affairs in which community of interest and individual interest are merely different aspects of the same thing."[19]

Now, the Church maintains that respect for this second principle bears certain concrete implications as far as economic life is concerned.

To begin with, the right economic system would be the one which can ensure that every individual in an economic association will have easy access to the goods and services he requires in order to survive and flourish. The economic system must respect the fact that the goods of creation are intended to promote the benefit of each and every human person. This teaching is referred to as the universal destination of goods:

> **The original source of all that is good is the very act of God, who created both the earth and man, and who gave the earth to man so that he might have dominion over it by his work and enjoy its fruits (Gen 1:28). God gave the earth to the whole human race for the sustenance of all its members, without excluding or favouring anyone. This is *the foundation of the universal destination of the earth's goods*. The earth, by reason of its fruitfulness and its capacity to satisfy human needs, is God's first gift for the sustenance of human life.** *Centesimus Annus*, n. 31.

Accordingly, the adequate fulfillment of the true purpose of economic association (as defined both by Social Credit theory and Catholic social doctrine) must take precedence over other considerations when it comes to the design of an economic system:

> **If the world is made to furnish each individual with the means of livelihood and the instruments for his growth and progress, each man has therefore the right to find in the world what is necessary for himself. The recent Council reminded us of this:**

> "God intended the earth and all that it contains for the use of every human being and people. Thus, as all men follow justice and unite in charity, created goods should abound for them on a reasonable basis"[20]. All other rights whatsoever, including those of property and of free commerce, are to be subordinated to this principle. They should not hinder but on the contrary favor its application. It is a grave and urgent social duty to redirect them to their primary finality. *Populorum Progressio,* n. 22.

The right to private property (subject to the limitation just mentioned) is another one of the concrete implications bound up with respect for the common good in the economic sphere. The Church favours the widespread distribution of private property (over either private property monopolies or collectivistic common ownership) as the best general means for ensuring that the true purpose of economic association is adequately fulfilled. The Compendium of the Church's social doctrine defends this position in the following manner:

> Private property and other forms of private ownership of goods "assure a person a highly necessary sphere for the exercise of his personal and family autonomy and ought to be considered as an extension of human freedom ... stimulating exercise of responsibility, it constitutes one of the conditions for civil liberty."[369] Private property is an essential element of an authentically social and democratic economic policy, and it is the guarantee of a correct social order. *The Church's social doctrine requires that ownership of goods be equally accessible to all* [370], so that all may become, at least in some measure, owners, and it excludes recourse to forms of "common and promiscuous dominion" [371]. *Compendium of the Social Doctrine of the Church,* n. 176.

For his part, Douglas concurred with the Church's teaching on the importance of widely distributed property as well as with her reasoning:

> It is probably an indication of the extent to which the Church of England, regarded as an organisation, has become honeycombed by Freemasonic and Communistic ideas, that the Archbishop of York, in his enunciation of human rights, significantly omitted any reference to the right to own property – a right on which the Roman Catholic Church has always placed emphasis as a basis of freedom.[20]

3. **Subsidiarity** – *"Render therefore to Caesar the things that are Caesar's; and to God, the things that are God's."* (Matthew 22:21)

Generally speaking, the closer an association is to an individual the more *effectively* it can meet his needs in a personal way, i.e., in a manner that respects and promotes his unique individuality. In view of this reality, the principle of subsidiarity teaches that, because associations exist for the sake of the individuals who compose them, those associations which are closest to the individual should be allowed to fulfill their own true purposes (i.e., their particular manifestations of the common good) in service to their individual members by the larger and more powerful associations in society. The former must not be illegitimately interfered with or unduly hampered. Beyond that, the larger and more powerful groups actually have the obligation of doing everything they can to support the smaller associations in the fulfillment of their proper tasks.

Thus, the family must be permitted and empowered to do all that lies within its natural aptitudes to secure the well-being of its individual members. Only those things which are beyond the inherent capacity of the family to take care of should be handled by the local authorities. In the same way, local authorities should be supported to do everything they can to meet the needs of the community in such a way that only those necessary functions which are intrinsically beyond the capacity of the local community to deal with would be handled by a provincial, regional, or federal authority. Finally, only those tasks which cannot be competently fulfilled by any of the smaller social bodies should be handled by the nation-state.

In other words, the principle of subsidiarity stands for the greatest possible *decentralization* of political and economic power in the direction of the individual to the extent that the progressively smaller units of society can adequately fulfill the true purposes of the social order. No larger body should dominate or subsume the functions of the smaller by doing for the smaller what it can and should do for itself; any transgression of this order would be an abuse of the authority of the larger and more powerful body in the hierarchy of associations. The initiative, freedom, and responsibility of the smaller bodies must be scrupulously respected.[21] The principle of subsidiarity thus stands in stark contrast to the increasing economic and political centralization, i.e., the collectivistic tendencies, which characterize the modern world:

> **Just as it is gravely wrong to take from individuals what they can accomplish by their own initiative and industry and give it to the community, so also is it an injustice, and at the same time a grave evil and disturbance of right order, to assign to a greater and higher association what lesser and subordinate organizations can do. For every social activity ought of its very nature to furnish help to**

the members of the social body, and never destroy and absorb them. *Quadragessimo Anno, n. 79.*

Douglas' straightforward agreement with the principle of subsidiarity was most clearly and succinctly expressed in one of the first chapters of *Economic Democracy*:

[W]e must build up from the individual, not down from the State.[22]

Violations of the principle of subsidiarity basically fall into one of two categories: either the larger bodies unjustifiably interfere with the functioning of smaller bodies, or the larger bodies fail in their task of providing adequate support so that the smaller bodies can fulfill their specific functions well. By both eliminating the disordered and/or inordinate *meddling* of the higher bodies in the operation of the lower bodies and *requiring* that these higher bodies supply the necessary kind of assistance to the lower bodies (by insisting on and facilitating the proper fulfillment of the former's due functions), the Social Credit economic reforms would bring the economic order into far greater alignment with the principle of subsidiarity.

As far as the first type of violation is concerned, Social Credit would eliminate all of the forms of taxation which are inherently unjust. Take, for example, that proportion of taxation which represents servicing charges for chronic public debts which were created when the government borrowed credit from private banks instead of, for example, borrowing it interest free from a National Credit Office and then re-collectting the expenditures in full from taxpayers. Taxes to cover debt-servicing charges represent an unjustifiable imposition of the governmental authorities on the common members of an economic association for the benefit of the existing monopoly of credit. In a similar way, the implementation of the dividend, by eliminating the necessity of most social programmes and redistributive taxation, would also go a long way to lowering much of the remaining taxation, while at the same time reducing the size and power of government bureaucracy over people's lives.

Interestingly enough, the marked tendency of socialistic economic systems to violate subsidiarity by employing the very methods that Social Credit would eradicate has been recognized by the Church:

> **In recent years the range of such intervention [of the State – OH] has vastly expanded, to the point of creating a new type of State, the so-called 'Welfare State'. This has happened in some countries in order to respond better to many needs and demands, by remedying forms of poverty and deprivation unworthy of the human person. However, excesses and abuses, especially in recent years, have provoked very harsh criticism of the Welfare State, dubbed the 'Social Assistance State'. Malfunctions and defects in the Social Assistance State are the result of an inadequate understanding of the tasks proper to the State. Here again *the principle of subsidiarity* must be respected: a community of higher order should not interfere in the internal life of a community of a lower order, depriving the latter of its functions, but rather should support it in case of need and help to coordinate its activity with the activities of the rest of society, always with a view to the common good.**
>
> **By intervening directly and depriving society of its responsibility, the Social Assistance State leads to a loss of human energy and an inordinate increase of public agencies, which are dominated more by bureaucratic ways of**

thinking than by concern for serving their clients, and which are accompanied by an enormous increase in spending. *Centesimus Annus,* n. 48.

Positively speaking, by providing a dividend to each of its members, a Social Credit state would be in a position to provide substantial support to the family (which has been recognized by the Church as the basic social unit of society at large). It would, for example, allow for the work done by mothers in the home to be economically and hence socially recognized and recompensed. This is one of the achievements which the Church has recognized as a mark of a just social order:

> Experience confirms that there must be a *social re-evaluation of the mother's role*, of the toil connected with it, and of the need that children have for care, love and affection in order that they may develop into responsible, morally and religiously mature and psychologically stable persons. It will redound to the credit of society to make it possible for a mother – without inhibiting her freedom, without psychological or practical discrimination, and without penalizing her as compared with other women – to devote herself to taking care of her children and educating them in accordance with their needs, which vary with age. Having to abandon these tasks in order to take up paid work outside the home is wrong from the point of view of the good of society and of the family when it contradicts or hinders these primary goals of the mission of a mother. *Laborem Excercens,* n. 19.[23]

As far as the second basic way in which the principle of subsidiarity can be violated, i.e., the failure of a larger social body to fulfill those specific functions which it alone is in a position to undertake, Social Credit would require the state to properly identify and adequately fulfill those functions that uniquely fall within its jurisdiction. Regulating a country's financial system in the true interests of the common good certainly qualifies as one of those tasks which falls to the state.[24] Douglas' economic reforms would make up for the present negligence by instituting a politically independent 'National Credit Office' to impartially regulate the financial parameters of the economic system in accordance with the correct set of principles so that a condition of financial sufficiency and homeostasis can be attained.

4. Solidarity – *"[A]s long as you did to one of these my least brethren, you did it to me."* (Matthew 25:40)

The fourth and final principle, i.e., the principle of solidarity, may be thought of as a stipulation which is necessary in order to prevent the principle of subsidiarity from being misinterpreted, i.e., interpreted in such a way that its application would interfere with the pursuit of the common good. It qualifies the principle of subsidiarity by indicating that the sort of decentralization which subsidiarity champions cannot be of the nature or degree that would allow certain individuals or groups to profit at the illegitimate expense of weaker individuals or groups.[25] On the contrary, all must benefit equitably (not necessarily equally) from the ordered progress of society. No man exists as a self-sufficient island; we are all interdependent when we live in society and we must therefore ensure that the common rules by which we live protect the legitimate rights of each and every individual and of the natural environment upon which we all rely. This implies common duties and responsibilities. By respecting these social requirements in their very structures, the economic and political systems, etc., can embody a commitment to the good of each and every individual member which will yield consonant results. Solidarity is thus at odds with any radical or extreme individualism which would fail to do full justice to the authentic functional necessities of human association.

Douglas also accepted the validity and importance of the principle of solidarity in the social order. On one occasion he described the Social Credit vision of society as follows:

> **First of all, it** [the supremacy of the individual considered collectively, over any external interest - OH] **does *not* mean anarchy, nor does it mean exactly what is commonly called individualism, which generally resolves itself into a claim to force the individuality of others to subordinate itself to the will-to-power of the self-styled individualist.**[26]

Negatively speaking, the reforms of Social Credit are in line with the principle of solidarity because, by eliminating the monopoly of credit and balancing the flow of final prices with adequate consumer purchasing power, they would also eliminate the financial exploitation and manipulation to which we are all subject, but which is particularly burdensome where the economically vulnerable are concerned. No longer would an elite group of financiers be in a position to usurp the unearned increment of economic association in their own interests and at the illegitimate expense of the rest of us. Economic solidarity demands that economic life operate in keeping with the principles and spirit of 'fair play', and Social Credit would do much to establish this level playing field.

Beyond this, the most obvious indication that Social Credit economic theory fully embodies the principle of solidarity is the fact that it mandates that each individual should be granted a share in the communal profit in the form of a National Dividend – whether they be employed or not. In a modern, industrialized state this should be (in conjunction with the compensated price) sufficient to eliminate poverty and to provide individuals with a constructive economic platform on the basis of which they may then proceed to construct a meaningful and fulfilling life. There could be no greater method of establishing solidarity as a concrete reality in economic association than by recognizing a certain basic economic independence, security, and freedom (in the form of the dividend) as an unconditional social right of each and every citizen in perpetuity.

In pondering the various implications of this fourth and final principle, it should also be pointed out that it is on account of solidarity that Catholics (and indeed all men of good will) have a serious moral obligation to search for better economic and political systems. Once these have been found, solidarity also demands that people make them widely known and that they work effectively for their introduction:

> **The principle of solidarity, in a wide sense, must inspire the effective search for appropriate institutions and mechanisms ... This difficult road of the indispensable transformation of the structures of economic life is one on which it will not be easy to go forward without the intervention of a true conversion of mind, will and heart. The task requires resolute commitment by individuals and peoples that are free and linked in solidarity.**[27]
> *Redemptor Hominis*, n. 16.

In the opinion of the present author, adhesion to the Social Credit movement is, from this particular point of view, the best way of putting the principle of solidarity into action.

Concluding Summary

On the basis of the foregoing comparative study, would it be too much to say that the Church's social teachings would be most perfectly embodied on the economic plane by the Social Credit remedial proposals in comparison with various other alternatives? And if we hold that the Church's social teachings comprise the correct set of social principles, would it not then follow that the economic system which best puts these truths into practice must, of necessity, share in that 'rightness'? Does the acceptance of the validity of the social teachings of the Church not then imply, once the relevant evidence has been gathered and properly assessed, the acceptance of Social Credit?

The Views of Douglas on the Economic Implications of Christianity:

Douglas was certainly of the belief that there was a deep connection between the social dimensions of the Christian *Weltanschauung* and Social Credit that went beyond mere compatibility. Christianity seemed to imply the sort of economic system which would constitute a direct challenge, based on an appeal to the authentic common good, to the prevailing oligarchic powers, just as Social Credit does in fact so challenge them:

[W]ithout pretending to be an authority on these matters, I am fairly confident that the persecution which was the lot of Christianity in its earliest years was by no means because it was concerned with something purely transcendental – something that we call the world to come. Taking the merely material implications in it, I have little doubt that what was recognised and persecuted in early Christianity was the economic implications of its philosophy. Only when Christianity became, as it did, purely transcendentalist, was it felt to be fairly respectable and fairly safe.[28]

The Views of Catholics on the Religious Implications of Social Credit

Over the years many Catholics (including the present author) have likewise become convinced that the compelling promise of the Church's social teachings can only – within the context of a modern, industrialized economy – be brought to a spectacular fulfillment through the application of Social Credit techniques. These would allow the economic system to operate in the service of man by adequately facilitating the fulfillment of the true purpose of economic association. Some prominent Catholics who were also Social Credit supporters or at least sympathizers included a number of priests, such as Father Coffey (Professor at Maynooth College, Ireland), Father Drinkwater, and Father Watt, S.J., as well as lay people, such as Anthony Cooney, J. Ernest Grégoire (former Mayor of Québec City and member of the Québec Legislative Assembly), Christopher Hollis, and Louis Even.[29] In close collaboration with Gilberte Coté-Mercier and Gérard Mercier, the latter went on to found an extensive lay movement dedicated to the promotion of the Social Credit cause. This movement, known as the

Pilgrims of Saint Michael, remains active to the present day. Other Catholics, such as the famous French Thomist Jacques Maritain, worked independently on other lines which are at least partially parallel to Social Credit thinking.[30] More recently, clerical supporters of Social Credit have included Cardinal Bernard Agré, Bishop Zbigniew Kraszewski, and Msgr. Edward Frankowski, amongst several others. The present chairwoman of Douglas' Social Credit Secretariat, Frances Hutchinson, is a convert to Catholicism.

In seeking to do justice to this particular subject, it is important to note that many high-church Anglicans or Anglo-Catholics have also been ardent Social Crediters. In spite of their theological deviations from Rome, these Christians share the underlying sociology and basic view of man inherent to Catholicity. Leading Anglo-Catholic supporters or sympathizers included Fr. V.A. Demant, T.S. Eliot, T.M. Heron, Dr. Hewlett Johnson (for a certain period of time), the Reverend W.G. Peck, M.B. Reckitt, the Reverend P.E.T. Widdrington, and, to a certain extent and at least ostensibly, William Temple, the Archbishop of Canterbury.[31]

Indeed, the kind and degree of alignment existing between Catholic social teaching and Social Credit economics (a similar parallel can be drawn between the Church's social doctrine and Social Credit political theory) is so astonishingly great that whoever it was who first described Social Credit as a form of 'practical' or 'applied' Christianity was certainly correct.

The Views of Various Popes on Social Credit Themes:

Could it be the case that some of the Catholic enthusiasts for Social Credit might even have been Popes? It has been reported that in 1950 a group of businessmen in Québec had asked Bishop Albertus Martin of Nicolet to visit Rome with the objective of obtaining a formal condemnation of Social Credit. Upon his return, the Bishop told the businessman the following: "If you want to get a condemnation of Social Credit it is not to Rome that you must go. Pius XII said to me: 'Social Credit would create, in the world, a climate that would allow [for] the blossoming of [the] family and Christianity.' "[32]

While not explicitly endorsing Social Credit by name, there are, as a matter of fact, a number of public, authoritative declarations which have been made by various Popes throughout the ages and more especially since 1917 (the year in which Douglas began to formulate his Social Credit ideas) which seem to point the Church's faithful in an unmistakably Social Credit direction. The following citations, the majority of which have been pulled from encyclicals, provide key lines of orientation which, when taken together as a whole, look broadly and prophetically like a description of the Social Credit economic order.

On the legitimacy of the normative and on its priority over the descriptive in economics:

> Even though economics and moral science employs each its own principles in its own sphere, it is, nevertheless, an error to say that the economic and moral orders are so distinct from and alien to each other that the former depends in no way on the latter. Certainly the laws of economics, as they are termed, being based on the very nature of material things and on the capacities of the human body and mind, determine the limits of what productive human effort cannot, and of what it can attain in the economic field and by what means. Yet it is reason itself that clearly shows, on the basis of the individual and social nature

of things and of men, the purpose which God ordained for all economic life. *Quadragesimo Anno*, n. 42.

The economy needs ethics in order to function correctly — not any ethics whatsoever, but an ethics which is people-centred. Veritas in Caritate, n. 45.

On the true purpose of economic association:

For then only will the social economy be rightly established and attain its purposes when all and each are supplied with all the goods that the wealth and resources of nature, technical achievement, and the social organization of economic life can furnish. And these goods ought indeed to be enough both to meet the demands of necessity and decent comfort and to advance people to that happier and fuller condition of life which, when it is wisely cared for, is not only no hindrance to virtue but helps it greatly.[47] *Quadragesimo Anno*, n. 75.

All of you who have heard the appeal of suffering peoples, all of you who are working to answer their cries, you are the apostles of a development which is good and genuine, which is not wealth that is self-centred and sought for its own sake, but rather an economy which is put at the service of man, the bread which is daily distributed to all, as a source of brotherhood and a sign of Providence. *Populorum Progressio*, n. 86.

Economics and technology have no meaning except from man whom they should serve. *Populorum Progressio*, n. 34.

[T]he aim of a just social order is to guarantee to each person, according to the principle of subsidiarity, his share of the community's goods. This has always been emphasized by Christian teaching on the State and by the Church's social doctrine. *Deus Caritas Est*, n. 26.

On the falseness of the labour theory of value:

For they are greatly in error who do not hesitate to spread the principle that labor is worth and must be paid as much as its products are worth, and that consequently the one who hires out his labor has the right to demand all that is produced through his labor. How far this is from the truth is evident from that We have already explained in treating of property and labor. *Quadragesimo Anno*, n. 68.

On the cultural heritage as a factor of production:

The present historical period has placed at the disposal of society new goods that were completely unknown until recent times. This calls for a fresh reading of the principle of the universal destination of the goods of the earth and makes it necessary to extend this principle so that it includes the latest developments brought about by economic and technological progress. The ownership of the new goods – the results of knowledge, technology and know-how – becomes ever more decisive, because "the wealth of the industrialized nations is based much more on this kind of ownership than on natural resources." [379]. *Compendium of the Social Doctrine of the Church*, n. 179.

Working at any workbench, whether a relatively primitive or an ultramodern one, a man can easily see that *through his work he enters into two inheritances*: the inheritance of what is given to the whole of humanity in the resources of nature, and the inheritance of what others have already developed on the basis of those resources, primarily by developing technology, that is to say, by producing a whole collection of increasingly perfect instruments for work. In working, man also "enters into the labour of others." *Laborem Exercens*, n. 13.

On the paradox of poverty amidst plenty:

It is a cruel paradox that many of you who could be engaged in the production of food are in financial distress here, while at the same time hunger, chronic malnutrition and the threat of starvation afflict millions of people elsewhere in the world. John Paul II to the fishermen of Newfoundland on Sept. 12, 1984.[33]

On the technical defects at the root of economic failure:

No more hunger, hunger never again! Ladies and gentlemen, this objective can be achieved. The threat of starvation and the weight of malnutrition are not an inescapable fate. Nature is not, in this crisis, unfaithful to man. According to a generally accepted opinion, while 50% of cultivable land is not yet developed, a great scandal catches the eye from the huge amount of surplus food that certain countries periodically destroy for lack of a sound economy which would have ensured a useful consumption of this food.

Here we are broaching the paradox of the present situation: Mankind has an incomparable control over the universe; it possesses instruments capable of exploiting its natural resources at full capacity. Will the owners of these instruments remain paralyzed and stuck in front of the absurdity of a situation where the wealth of the few tolerates the persistent extreme poverty of the many? ... We cannot arrive at such a situation without having committed serious errors of orientation, be it sometimes through negligence or omission; it is high time we discovered how the mechanisms are defective, in order to correct, put the whole situation right. Message of Paul VI to the World Conference of Food in Rome on Nov. 9th, 1974.

It is obvious that a fundamental defect, or rather a series of defects, indeed a defective machinery is at the root of contemporary economics and materialistic civilization, which does not allow the human family to break free from such radically unjust situations. *Dives in Misericordia*, n. 11.

Hunger is not so much dependent on lack of material things as on shortage of social resources, the most important of which are institutional. What is missing, in other words, is a network of economic institutions capable of guaranteeing regular access to sufficient food and water for nutritional needs, and also capable of addressing the primary needs and necessities ensuing from genuine food crises, whether due to natural causes or political irresponsibility, nationally and internationally. The problem of food insecurity needs to be addressed within a long-term perspective, eliminating the structural causes that give rise to it and promoting the agricultural development of poorer countries. *Caritas in Veritate,* n. 27.

On the primarily financial nature of the technical economic defects:

Indeed everyone is familiar with the picture of the consumer civilization, which consists in a certain surplus of goods necessary for man and for entire societies – and we are dealing precisely with the rich highly developed societies – while the remaining societies – at least broad sectors of them – are suffering from hunger, with many people dying each day of starvation and malnutrition. Hand in hand go a certain abuse of freedom by one group – an abuse linked precisely with a consumer attitude uncontrolled by ethics – and a limitation by it of the freedom of the others, that is to say those suffering marked shortages and being driven to conditions of even worse misery and destitution.

This pattern, which is familiar to all, and the contrast referred to, in the documents giving their teaching, by the Popes of this century, most recently by John XXIII and by Paul VI [104] represent, as it were, the gigantic development of the parable in the Bible of the rich banqueter and the poor man Lazarus [105]. *So widespread is the phenomenon that it brings into question the financial, monetary, production and commercial mechanisms that, resting on various political pressures, support the world economy. These are proving incapable either of remedying the unjust social situations inherited from the past or of dealing with the urgent challenges and ethical demands of the present.* By submitting man to tensions created by himself, dilapidating at an accelerated pace material and energy resources, and compromising the geophysical environment, these structures unceasingly make the areas of misery spread, accompanied by anguish, frustration and bitterness. *Redemptor Hominis*, n. 16. [emphasis mine]

On the lack of purchasing power:

It would appear that, on the level of individual nations and of international relations, the *free market* is the most efficient instrument for utilizing resources and effectively responding to needs. But this is true only for those needs which are "solvent", insofar as they are endowed with purchasing power, and for those resources which are "marketable", insofar as they are capable of obtaining a satisfactory price. But there are many human needs which find no place on the market. It is a strict duty of justice and truth not to allow fundamental human needs to remain unsatisfied, and not to allow those burdened by such needs to perish. *Centesimus Annus*, n. 34.

On the immorality of the oligarchic principle in human affairs:

[A]mong the actions and attitudes opposed to the will of God, the good of neighbour and the "structures" created by them, two are very typical: on the one hand, the all-consuming desire for profit, and on the other, the thirst for power, with the intention of imposing one's will upon others. In order to characterize better each of these attitudes, one can add the expression: "at any price".
Sollicitudo Rei Socialis, n. 37.

Less human conditions: oppressive social structures, whether due to the abuses of ownership or to the abuses of power.... *Populorum Progressio*, n. 21.

The decisions which create a human environment can give rise to specific structures of sin which impede the full realization of those who are in any way oppressed by them. To destroy such structures and replace them with more authentic forms of living in community is a task which demands courage and patience. *Centesimus Annus*, n. 38.

On the immorality of the credit monopoly in particular:

In the first place, it is obvious that not only is wealth concentrated in our times but an immense power and despotic economic dictatorship is consolidated in the hands of a few, who often are not owners but only the trustees and managing directors of invested funds which they administer according to their own arbitrary will and pleasure.

This dictatorship is being most forcibly exercised by those who, since they hold the money and completely control it, control credit also and rule the lending of money. Hence they regulate the flow, so to speak, of the lifeblood whereby the entire economic system lives, and have so firmly in their grasp the soul, as it were, of economic life that no one can breathe against their will.

This concentration of power and might, the characteristic mark, as it were, of contemporary economic life, is the fruit that the unlimited freedom of struggle among competitors has of its own nature produced, and which lets only the strongest survive; and this is often the same as saying, those who fight the most violently, those who give least heed to their conscience. *Quadragesimo Anno*, nn. 105-107.

[O]ne must denounce the existence of economic, financial and social mechanisms which, although they are manipulated by people, often function almost automatically, thus accentuating the situation of wealth for some and poverty for the rest. *Sollicitudo Rei Socialis*, n. 16.

However, certain concepts have somehow arisen out of these new conditions and insinuated themselves into the fabric of human society. These concepts present profit as the chief spur to economic progress, free competition as the guiding norm of economics, and private ownership of the means of production as an absolute right, having no limits nor concomitant social obligations. This unbridled liberalism paves the way for a particular type of tyranny, rightly condemned by Our predecessor Pius XI, for it results in the "international imperialism of money."(26) Such improper manipulations of economic forces can never be condemned enough; let it be said once again that economics is supposed to be in the service of man. (27)But if it is true that a type of capitalism, as it is commonly called, has given rise to hardships, unjust practices, and fratricidal conflicts that persist to this day, it would be a mistake to attribute these evils to the rise of industrialization itself, for they really derive from the pernicious economic concepts that grew up along with it. We must in all fairness acknowledge the vital role played by labor systemization and industrial organization in the task of development. *Populorum Progressio*, n. 26.

On usury and other dishonest profit:

I. The nature of the sin called usury has its proper place and origin in a loan contract. This financial contract between consenting parties demands, by its very nature, that one return to another only as much as he has received. The sin rests on the fact that sometimes the creditor desires more than he has given. Therefore he contends some gain is owed him beyond that which he loaned, but any gain which exceeds the amount he gave is illicit and usurious.

II. One cannot condone the sin of usury by arguing that the gain is not great or excessive, but rather moderate or small; neither can it be condoned by arguing that the borrower is rich; nor even by arguing that the money borrowed is not left idle, but is spent usefully, either to increase one's fortune, to purchase new estates, or to engage in business transactions. The law governing loans consists necessarily in the equality of what is given and returned; once the equality has been established, whoever demands more than that violates the terms of the loan. Therefore if one receives interest, he must make restitution according to the commutative bond of justice; its function in human contracts is to assure equality for each one. This law is to be observed in a holy manner. If not observed exactly, reparation must be made.

III. By these remarks, however, We do not deny that at times together with the loan contract certain other titles – which are not at all intrinsic to the contract – may run parallel with it. From these other titles, entirely just and legitimate reasons arise to demand something over and above the amount due on the contract. Nor is it denied that it is very often possible for someone, by means of contracts differing entirely from loans, to spend and invest money legitimately either to provide oneself with an annual income or to engage in legitimate trade and business. From these types of contracts honest gain may be made.

IV. There are many different contracts of this kind. In these contracts, if equality is not maintained, whatever is received over and above what is fair is a real injustice. Even though it may not fall under the precise rubric of usury (since all reciprocity, both open and hidden, is absent), restitution is obligated. Thus if everything is done correctly and weighed in the scales of justice, these same legitimate contracts suffice to provide a standard and a principle for engaging in commerce and fruitful business for the common good. Christian minds should not think that gainful commerce can flourish by usuries or other similar injustices. On the contrary We learn from divine Revelation that justice raises up nations; sin, however, makes nations miserable.

V. But you must diligently consider this, that some will falsely and rashly persuade themselves – and such people can be found anywhere – that together with loan contracts there are other legitimate titles or, excepting loan contracts, they might convince themselves that other just contracts exist, for which it is permissible to receive a moderate amount of interest. Should any one think like this, he will oppose not only the judgment of the Catholic Church on usury, but also common human sense and natural reason. Everyone knows that man is obliged in many instances to help his fellows with a simple, plain loan. Christ Himself teaches this: "Do not refuse to lend to him who asks you." In many circumstances, no other true and just contract may be possible except for a loan. Whoever therefore wishes to follow his conscience must first diligently inquire if, along with the loan, another category exists by means of which the gain he seeks may be lawfully attained."[34] *Vix Pervenit*, n. 3.

[B]y degrees it has come to pass that working men have been surrendered, isolated and helpless, to the hardheartedness of employers and the greed of unchecked competition. The mischief has been increased by rapacious usury, which, although more than once condemned by the Church, is nevertheless, under a different guise, but with like injustice, still practiced by covetous and grasping men. *Rerum Novarum*, n. 3.

Furthermore, the *experience of micro-finance*, which has its roots in the thinking and activity of the civil humanists — I am thinking especially of the birth of pawnbroking — should be strengthened and fine-tuned. This is all the more necessary in these days when financial difficulties can become severe for many of the more vulnerable sectors of the population, who should be protected from the risk of usury and from despair. The weakest members of society should be helped to defend themselves against usury, just as poor peoples should be helped to derive real benefit from micro-credit, in order to discourage the exploitation that is possible in these two areas. *Caritas in Veritate*, n. 65.

On the necessity of a new economic system:

I join with them [the Canadian Bishops - OH] in appealing to those in positions of responsibility, and to all involved, to work together to find appropriate solutions to the problems at hand, including a re-structuring of the economy, so that human needs be put before mere financial gain. The social doctrine of the Church requires us to emphasize the primacy of the human person in the productive process, the primacy of people over things. John Paul II in Newfoundland on Sept. 12, 1984.[35]

An essential condition is to provide the economy with a human meaning and logic. What I said with respect to work is also valid here. It is necessary to liberate the various fields of existence from the dominion of a subjugating economism. It is necessary to put economic requirements in their proper place and to create a multiform social fabric which will impede standardization. No one is dispensed from collaborating in this task ... Christians, in whichever place you happen to be, assume your share of responsibility in this immense effort for the human restructuring of the city. Faith makes it a duty. John Paul II to the workers of São Paulo, Brazil on June 3, 1980.[36] [my translation]

> Efforts are needed — and it is essential to say this — not only to create "ethical" sectors or segments of the economy or the world of finance, but to ensure that the whole economy — the whole of finance — is ethical, not merely by virtue of an external label, but *by its respect for requirements intrinsic to its very nature*. The Church's social teaching is quite clear on the subject, recalling that the economy, in all its branches, constitutes a sector of human activity. *Caritas in Veritate*, n. 45. [emphasis mine]

On the necessity of changing the financial system in order for the economy to fulfill its true purpose:

> I have to address a delicate and painful issue. I would like to speak of the torment experienced by the representatives of several countries who no longer know what to do in the face of the agonizing problem of indebtedness. Without wishing to enter into technical considerations, I would nevertheless like to mention this problem which constitutes one of the most complex aspects of the general situation of the international economy. A structural reform of the world financial system is, without any doubt, one of the most urgent and necessary initiatives. Message of Pope John Paul II to the 6th United Nations Conference on Trade and Development in Geneva, Switzerland on September 26th, 1985.[37] [my translation]

As a democratic society, see carefully to all that is happening in this powerful world of money! The world of finance is also a human world, our world, submitted to the conscience of all of us; for it too exist ethical principles. So see especially to it that you may bring a contribution to world peace with your economy and your banks and not a contribution – perhaps in an indirect way – to war and injustice! John Paul II homily at Flueli, Switzerland on June 14, 1984.

Finance, therefore — through the renewed structures and operating methods that have to be designed after its misuse, which wreaked such havoc on the real economy — now needs to go back to being an *instrument directed towards improved wealth creation and development*. Insofar as they are instruments, the entire economy and finance, not just certain sectors, must be used in an ethical way so as to create suitable conditions for human development and for the development of peoples. *Veritas in Caritate*, n. 65.

On the value of free enterprise:

It should be noted that in today's world, among other rights, the right of economic initiative is often suppressed. Yet it is a right which is important not only for the individual but also for the common good. Experience shows us that the denial of this right, or its limitation in the name of an alleged "equality" of everyone in society, diminishes, or in practice absolutely destroys the spirit of initiative, that is to say the creative subjectivity of the citizen. As a consequence, there arises, not so much a true

equality as a "leveling down." In the place of creative initiative there appears passivity, dependence and submission to the bureaucratic apparatus which, as the only "ordering" and "decision-making" body – if not also the "owner" – of the entire totality of goods and the means of production, puts everyone in a position of almost absolute dependence, which is similar to the traditional dependence of the worker-proletarian in capitalism.
Sollicitudo Rei Socialis, n. 15.

On the legitimacy of functionalist financial profit:

The Church acknowledges the legitimate *role of profit* as an indication that a business is functioning well. When a firm makes a profit, this means that productive factors have been properly employed and corresponding human needs have been duly satisfied. But profitability is not the only indicator of a firm's condition. It is possible for the financial accounts to be in order, and yet for the people — who make up the firm's most valuable asset — to be humiliated and their dignity offended. Besides being morally inadmissible, this will eventually have negative repercussions on the firm's economic efficiency. In fact, the purpose of a business firm is not simply to make a profit, but is to be found in its very existence as a *community of persons* who in various ways are endeavouring to satisfy their basic needs, and who form a particular group at the service of the whole of society. Profit is a regulator of the life of a business, but it is not the only one; *other human and moral factors* must also be considered which, in the long term, are at least equally important for the life of a business. *Centesimus Annus*, n. 35.

Profit is useful if it serves as a means towards an end that provides a sense both how to produce it and how to make good use of it. Once profit becomes the exclusive goal, if it is produced by improper means and without the common good as its ultimate end, it risks destroying wealth and creating poverty. *Caritas in Veritate*, n. 21.

On the priority of the fulfillment of the true purpose of economic association over and above negative economic freedoms:

If the world is made to furnish each individual with the means of livelihood and the instruments for his growth and progress, each man has therefore the right to find in the world what is necessary for himself. The recent Council reminded us of this: "God intended the earth and all that it contains for the use of every human being and people. Thus, as all men follow justice and unite in charity, created goods should abound for them on a reasonable basis"[20]. All other rights whatsoever, including those of property and of free commerce, are to be subordinated to this principle. They should not hinder but on the contrary favor its application. It is a grave and urgent social duty to redirect them to their primary finality. .... private property does not constitute for anyone an absolute and unconditioned right. ... In a word, "according to the traditional doctrine as found in the Fathers of the Church and the great theologians, the right to property must never be exercised to the detriment of the common good".
Populorum Progressio, nn. 22-23.

The teaching of Leo XIII in *Rerum Novarum* is always valid: if the positions of the contracting parties are too unequal, the consent of the parties does not suffice to guarantee the justice of their contract, and the rule of free agreement remains subservient to the demands of the natural law.[57] What was true of the just wage for the individual is also true of international contracts: an economy of exchange can no longer be based solely on the law of free competition, a law which, in its turn, too often creates an economic dictatorship. Freedom of trade is fair only if it is subject to the demands of social justice.
Populorum Progressio, n. 59.

In this area one cannot employ two systems of weights and measures. What holds for a national economy or among developed countries is valid also in commercial relations between rich nations and poor nations. Without abolishing the competitive market, it should be kept within the limits which make it just and moral, and therefore human. *Populorum Progressio,* n. 61.

In this sense, it is right to speak of a struggle against an economic system, if the latter is understood as a method of upholding the absolute predominance of capital, the possession of the means of production and of the land, in contrast to the free and personal nature of human work.[73] In the struggle against such a system, what is being proposed as an alternative is not the socialist system, which in fact turns out to be State capitalism, but rather *a society of free work, of enterprise and of participation.* Such a society is not directed against the market, but demands that the market be appropriately controlled by the forces of society and by the State, so as to guarantee that the basic needs of the whole of society are satisfied. *Centesimus Annus,* n. 35.

On the falseness of the conventional economic spectrum:

[T]he tension between East and West is not in itself an opposition between two different levels of development but rather between two concepts of the development of individuals and peoples, both concepts being imperfect and in need of radical correction ... This is one of the reasons why the Church's social doctrine adopts a critical attitude towards both liberal capitalism and Marxist collectivism. *Sollicitudo Rei Socialis,* n. 21.

Returning now to the initial question: can it perhaps be said that, after the failure of Communism, capitalism is the victorious social system, and that capitalism should be the goal of the countries now making efforts to rebuild their economy and society? Is this the model which ought to be proposed to the countries of the Third World which are searching for the path to true economic and civil progress?

The answer is obviously complex. If by "capitalism" is meant an economic system which recognizes the fundamental and positive role of business, the market, private property and the resulting responsibility for the means of production, as well as free human creativity in the economic sector, then the answer is certainly in the affirmative, even though it would perhaps be more appropriate to speak of a "business economy", "market economy " or simply "free economy". But if by "capitalism" is meant a system in which freedom in the economic sector is not circumscribed within a strong juridical framework which places it at the service of human freedom in its totality, and which sees it as a particular aspect of that freedom, the core of which is ethical and religious, then the reply is certainly negative.

The Marxist solution has failed, but the realities of marginalization and exploitation remain in the world, especially the Third World, as does the reality of human alienation, especially in the more advanced countries. Against these phenomena the Church strongly raises her voice. Vast multitudes are still living in conditions of great material and moral poverty. The collapse of the Communist system in so many countries certainly removes an obstacle to facing these problems in an appropriate and realistic way, but it is not enough to bring about their solution. Indeed, there is a risk that a radical capitalistic ideology could spread which refuses even to consider these problems, in the *a priori* belief that any attempt to solve them is doomed to failure, and which blindly entrusts their solution to the free development of market forces. *Centesimus Annus*, n. 42.

The Church has no models to present; models that are real and truly effective can only arise within the framework of different historical situations, through the efforts of all those who responsibly confront concrete problems in all their social, economic, political and cultural aspects, as these interact with one another.[84] For such a task the Church offers her social teaching as an *indispensable and ideal orientation,* a teaching which, as already mentioned, recognizes the positive value of the market and of enterprise, but which at the same time points out that these need to be oriented towards the common good. *Centesimus Annus*, n. 43.

Accordingly, twin rocks of shipwreck must be carefully avoided. For, as one is wrecked upon, or comes close to, what is known as "individualism" by denying or minimizing the social and public character of the right of property, so by rejecting or minimizing the private and individual character of this same right, one inevitably runs into "collectivism" or at least closely approaches its tenets. Unless this is kept in mind, one is swept from his course upon the shoals of that moral, juridical, and social modernism which We denounced in the Encyclical issued at the beginning of Our Pontificate.[29] *Quadragesimo Anno*, n. 46.

Attention must be given also to another matter that is closely connected with the foregoing. Just as the unity of human society cannot be founded on an opposition of classes, so also the right ordering of economic life cannot be left to a free competition of forces. For from this source, as from a poisoned spring, have originated and spread all the errors of individualist economic teaching. Destroying through forgetfulness or ignorance the social and moral character of economic life, it held that economic life must be considered and treated as altogether free from and independent of public authority, because in the market, i.e., in the free struggle of competitors, it would have a principle of self direction which governs it much more perfectly than would the intervention of any created intellect. But free competition, while justified and certainly useful provided it is kept within certain limits, clearly cannot direct economic life -- a truth which the outcome of the application in practice of the tenets of this evil individualistic spirit has more than sufficiently demonstrated. Therefore, it is most necessary that economic life be again subjected to and governed by a true and effective directing principle. This function is one that the economic dictatorship which has recently displaced free competition can still less perform, since it is a headstrong power and a violent energy that, to benefit people, needs to be strongly curbed and wisely ruled. But it cannot curb and rule itself. Loftier and nobler principles -- social justice and social charity -- must, therefore, be sought whereby this dictatorship may be governed firmly and fully. Hence, the institutions themselves of peoples and, particularly those of all social life, ought to be penetrated with this justice, and it is most necessary that it be truly effective, that is, establish a juridical and social order which will, as it were, give form and shape to all economic life. Social charity, moreover, ought to be as the soul of this order, an order which public authority ought to be ever ready effectively to protect and defend. *Quadragesimo Anno*, n. 88.

On the errors of capitalism:

>The ultimate consequences of the individualist spirit in economic life are those which you yourselves, Venerable Brethren and Beloved Children, see and deplore: Free competition has destroyed itself; economic dictatorship has supplanted the free market; unbridled ambition for power has likewise succeeded greed for gain; all economic life has become tragically hard, inexorable, and cruel. *Quadragesimo Anno,* n. 109.

>Strict and watchful moral restraint enforced vigorously by governmental authority could have banished these enormous evils and even forestalled them; this restraint, however, has too often been sadly lacking. For since the seeds of a new form of economy were bursting forth just when the principles of rationalism had been implanted and rooted in many minds, there quickly developed a body of economic teaching far removed from the true moral law, and, as a result, completely free rein was given to human passions.

>Thus it came to pass that many, much more than ever before, were solely concerned with increasing their wealth by any means whatsoever, and that in seeking their own selfish interests before everything else they had no conscience about committing even the gravest of crimes against others. Those first entering upon this broad way that leads to destruction[66] easily found numerous imitators of their iniquity by the example of their manifest success, by their insolent display of wealth, by their ridiculing the conscience of others, who, as they said, were troubled by silly scruples, or lastly by crushing

more conscientious competitors. *Quadragesimo Anno,* nn. 133-134.

On the inappropriateness of socialism as a solution to economic difficulties:

> To remedy these wrongs the socialists, working on the poor man's envy of the rich, are striving to do away with private property, and contend that individual possessions should become the common property of all, to be administered by the State or by municipal bodies. They hold that by thus transferring property from private individuals to the community, the present mischievous state of things will be set to rights, inasmuch as each citizen will then get his fair share of whatever there is to enjoy. But their contentions are so clearly powerless to end the controversy that were they carried into effect the working man himself would be among the first to suffer. They are, moreover, emphatically unjust, for they would rob the lawful possessor, distort the functions of the State, and create utter confusion in the community.
>
> It is surely undeniable that, when a man engages in remunerative labor, the impelling reason and motive of his work is to obtain property, and thereafter to hold it as his very own. If one man hires out to another his strength or skill, he does so for the purpose of receiving in return what is necessary for the satisfaction of his needs; he therefore expressly intends to acquire a right full and real, not only to the remuneration, but also to the disposal of such remuneration, just as he pleases. Thus, if he lives sparingly, saves money, and, for greater security, invests his savings in land, the land, in such case, is only his wages under another form; and, consequently, a working

man's little estate thus purchased should be as completely at his full disposal as are the wages he receives for his labor. But it is precisely in such power of disposal that ownership obtains, whether the property consist of land or chattels. Socialists, therefore, by endeavoring to transfer the possessions of individuals to the community at large, strike at the interests of every wage-earner, since they would deprive him of the liberty of disposing of his wages, and thereby of all hope and possibility of increasing his resources and of bettering his condition in life. ...

And in addition to injustice, it is only too evident what an upset and disturbance there would be in all classes, and to how intolerable and hateful a slavery citizens would be subjected. The door would be thrown open to envy, to mutual invective, and to discord; the sources of wealth themselves would run dry, for no one would have any interest in exerting his talents or his industry; and that ideal equality about which they entertain pleasant dreams would be in reality the leveling down of all to a like condition of misery and degradation. Hence, it is clear that the main tenet of socialism, community of goods, must be utterly rejected, since it only injures those whom it would seem meant to benefit, is directly contrary to the natural rights of mankind, and would introduce confusion and disorder into the commonweal. The first and most fundamental principle, therefore, if one would undertake to alleviate the condition of the masses, must be the inviolability of private property. This being established, we proceed to show where the remedy sought for must be found. *Rerum Novarum*, nn. 4-5, 15.

Pope Leo foresaw the negative consequences — political, social and economic — of the social order proposed by "socialism", ... Two things must be emphasized here: first, the great clarity in perceiving, in all its harshness, the actual condition of the working class — men, women and children; secondly, equal clarity in recognizing the evil of a solution which, by appearing to reverse the positions of the poor and the rich, was in reality detrimental to the very people whom it was meant to help. The remedy would prove worse than the sickness. By defining the nature of the socialism of his day as the suppression of private property, Leo XIII arrived at the crux of the problem. *Centessimus Annus*, n. 12.

On the incompatibility of socialism with Christianity:

But what if Socialism has really been so tempered and modified as to the class struggle and private ownership that there is in it no longer anything to be censured on these points? Has it thereby renounced its contradictory nature to the Christian religion? This is the question that holds many minds in suspense. And numerous are the Catholics who, although they clearly understand that Christian principles can never be abandoned or diminished seem to turn their eyes to the Holy See and earnestly beseech Us to decide whether this form of Socialism has so far recovered from false doctrines that it can be accepted without the sacrifice of any Christian principle and in a certain sense be baptized. That We, in keeping with Our fatherly solicitude, may answer their petitions, We make this pronouncement: Whether considered as a doctrine, or an historical fact, or a movement, Socialism, if it remains truly Socialism, even after it has yielded to truth and justice on the points which we have mentioned, cannot be reconciled with the teachings of the Catholic

Church because its concept of society itself is utterly foreign to Christian truth.

For, according to Christian teaching, man, endowed with a social nature, is placed on this earth so that by leading a life in society and under an authority ordained of God[54] he may fully cultivate and develop all his faculties unto the praise and glory of his Creator; and that by faithfully fulfilling the duties of his craft or other calling he may obtain for himself temporal and at the same time eternal happiness. Socialism, on the other hand, wholly ignoring and indifferent to this sublime end of both man and society, affirms that human association has been instituted for the sake of material advantage alone.

Because of the fact that goods are produced more efficiently by a suitable division of labor than by the scattered efforts of individuals, socialists infer that economic activity, only the material ends of which enter into their thinking, ought of necessity to be carried on socially. Because of this necessity, they hold that men are obliged, with respect to the producing of goods, to surrender and subject themselves entirely to society. Indeed, possession of the greatest possible supply of things that serve the advantages of this life is considered of such great importance that the higher goods of man, liberty not excepted, must take a secondary place and even be sacrificed to the demands of the most efficient production of goods. This damage to human dignity, undergone in the "socialized" process of production, will be easily offset, they say, by the abundance of socially produced goods which will pour out in profusion to individuals to be used freely at their pleasure for comforts and cultural development. Society, therefore, as Socialism conceives it, can on the one hand neither exist nor be thought of without an obviously excessive use of force; on the other hand, it fosters a liberty no less false, since there is no place in it for true social authority, which rests not on temporal and material advantages but descends from God alone, the Creator and last end of all things.[55]

If Socialism, like all errors, contains some truth (which, moreover, the Supreme Pontiffs have never denied), it is based nevertheless on a theory of human society peculiar to itself and irreconcilable with true Christianity. Religious socialism, Christian socialism, are contradictory terms; no one can be at the same time a good Catholic and a true socialist. *Quadragesimo Anno*, nn. 117-120.

On the doctrine of class struggle:

The great mistake made in regard to the matter now under consideration is to take up with the notion that class is naturally hostile to class, and that the wealthy and the working men are intended by nature to live in mutual conflict. So irrational and so false is this view that the direct contrary is the truth. Just as the symmetry of the human frame is the result of the suitable arrangement of the different parts of the body, so in a State is it ordained by nature that these two classes should dwell in harmony and agreement, so as to maintain the balance of the body politic. Each needs the other: capital cannot do without labor, nor labor without capital. Mutual agreement results in the beauty of good order, while perpetual conflict necessarily produces confusion and savage barbarity. *Rerum Novarum*, n. 19.

> First and foremost, the State and every good citizen ought to look to and strive toward this end: that the conflict between the hostile classes be abolished and harmonious cooperation of the Industries and Professions be encouraged and promoted. *Quadragesimo Anno*, n. 81.

On the Church's social doctrine as a higher synthesis which lies beyond the conventional economic and political spectra:

> The Church's social doctrine is not a "third way" between liberal capitalism and Marxist collectivism, nor even a possible alternative to other solutions less radically opposed to one another: rather, it constitutes a category of its own. *Sollicitudo Rei Socialis*, n. 41.

On the right to private property:

> [E]very man has by nature the right to possess property as his own. *Rerum Novarum*, n. 6.

> That the State is not permitted to discharge its duty arbitrarily is, however, clear. The natural right itself both of owning goods privately and of passing them on by inheritance ought always to remain intact and inviolate, since this indeed is a right that the State cannot take away: "For man is older than the State,"[34] and also "domestic living together is prior both in thought and in fact to uniting into a polity."[35] *Quadragesimo Anno*, n. 49.

The right of private ownership of goods, including productive goods, has permanent validity. It is part of the natural order, which teaches that the individual is prior to society and society must be ordered to the good of the individual.

Moreover, it would be quite useless to insist on free and personal initiative in the economic field, while at the same time withdrawing man's right to dispose freely of the means indispensable to the achievement of such initiative.

Further, history and experience testify that in those political regimes which do not recognize the rights of private ownership of goods, productive included, the exercise of freedom in almost every other direction is suppressed or stifled. This suggests, surely, that the exercise of freedom finds its guarantee and incentive in the right of ownership.

This explains why social and political movements for the harmonizing of justice and freedom in society, though until recently opposed to the private ownership of productive goods, are today reconsidering their position in the light of a clearer understanding of social history, and are in fact now declaring themselves in favor of this right.

Accordingly, We make Our own the directive of Our Predecessor Pius XII: "In defending the principle of private ownership the Church is striving after an important ethico-social end. She does not intend merely to uphold the present condition of things as if it were an expression of the divine Will, or to protect on principle the rich and plutocrats against the poor and indigent. . . The Church aims rather at securing that the institution of private property be such as it should be according to the plan of the divine Wisdom and the dispositions of Nature." (32) Hence private ownership must be considered as a guarantee of the essential freedom of the individual, and at the same time an indispensable element in a true social order. *Mater et Magistra*, nn. 109-111.

On the necessary orientation of private property towards the common good:

Finally, it is opportune to point out that the right to own private property entails a social obligation as well. *Pacem in Terris*, n. 22.

The above principle, as it was then stated and as it is still taught by the Church, *diverges* radically from the programme of *collectivism* as proclaimed by Marxism and put into practice in various countries in the decades following the time of Leo XIII's Encyclical. At the same time it differs from the programme of *capitalism* practised by liberalism and by the political systems inspired by it. In the latter case, the difference consists in the way the right to ownership or property is understood. Christian tradition has never upheld this right as absolute and untouchable. On the contrary, it has always understood this right within the broader context of the right common to all to use the goods of the whole of creation: *the right to private property is subordinated to the right to common use,* to the fact that goods are meant for everyone. *Laborem Exercens*, n. 14.

On the necessity of the widespread distribution of private property as part of an improved economic system:

> But it is not enough to assert that the right to own private property and the means of production is inherent in human nature. We must also insist on the extension of this right in practice to all classes of citizens.
>
> As our Predecessor Pius XII so rightly affirmed: the dignity of the human person "normally demands the right to the use of the goods of the earth, to which corresponds the fundamental obligation of granting an opportunity to possess property to all if possible." (33) This demand arises from the moral dignity of work. It also guarantees "the conservation and perfection of a social order which makes possible a secure, even if modest, property to all classes of people." (34)
>
> Now, if ever, is the time to insist on a more widespread distribution of property, in view of the rapid economic development of an increasing number of States. It will not be difficult for the body politic, by the adoption of various techniques of proved efficiency, to pursue an economic and social policy which facilitates the widest possible distribution of private property in terms of durable consumer goods, houses, land, tools and equipment (in the case of craftsmen and owners of family farms), and shares in medium and large business concerns."

Mater et Magistra, nn. 113-115.

The law, therefore, should favour ownership, and its policy should be to induce as many of the people as possible to become owners.

Many excellent results will follow from this; and, first of all, property will certainly become more equitably divided. ... A further consequence [of more equitably distributed private property - OH] will result in the great abundance of the fruits of the earth. Men always work harder and more readily when they work on that which belongs to them; nay, they learn to love the very soil that yields in response to the labor of their hands, not only food to eat, but an abundance of good things for themselves and those that are dear to them. That such a spirit of willing labor would add to the produce of the earth and to the wealth of the community is self-evident. *Rerum Novarum*, nn. 46, 47.

On a cure for the forced displacement of persons

And a third advantage [of more equitably distributed forms of private property - OH] would spring from this: men would cling to the country in which they were born, for no one would exchange his country for a foreign land if his own afforded him the means of living a decent and happy life. *Rerum Novarum*, 47.

On an equitable (not necessarily equal) distribution of wealth:

> But not every distribution among human beings of property and wealth is of a character to attain either completely or to a satisfactory degree of perfection the end which God intends. Therefore, the riches that economic-social developments constantly increase ought to be so distributed among individual persons and classes that the common advantage of all, which Leo XIII had praised, will be safeguarded; in other words, that the common good of all society will be kept inviolate. By this law of social justice, one class is forbidden to exclude the other from sharing in the benefits. Hence the class of the wealthy violates this law no less, when, as if free from care on account of its wealth, it thinks it the right order of things for it to get everything and the worker nothing, than does the non-owning working class when, angered deeply at outraged justice and too ready to assert wrongly the one right it is conscious of, it demands for itself everything as if produced by its own hands, and attacks and seeks to abolish, therefore, all property and returns or incomes, of whatever kind they are or whatever the function they perform in human society, that have not been obtained by labor, and for no other reason save that they are of such a nature." *Quadragesimo Anno*, n. 57.

> [T]he riches which are so abundantly produced in our age of "industrialism," as it is called, are not rightly distributed and equitably made available to the various classes of the people. *Quadragesimo Anno*, n. 60.

On the due limits of public ownership:

> State and public ownership of property is very much on the increase today. This is explained by the exigencies of the common good, which demand that public authority broaden its sphere of activity. But here, too, the "principle of subsidiary function" must be observed. The State and other agencies of public law must not extend their ownership of the common good properly understood, and even then there must be safeguards. Otherwise private ownership could be reduced beyond measure, or, even worse, completely destroyed. *Mater et Magistra,* n. 117.

On the immorality of oppressive levels of taxation:

> Wherefore the wise Pontiff declared that it is grossly unjust for a State to exhaust private wealth through the weight of imposts and taxes. "For since the right of possessing goods privately has been conferred not by man's law, but by nature, public authority cannot abolish it, but can only control its exercise and bring it into conformity with the common weal."[36] Yet when the State brings private ownership into harmony with the needs of the common good, it does not commit a hostile act against private owners but rather does them a friendly service; for it thereby effectively prevents the private possession of goods, which the Author of nature in His most wise providence ordained for the support of human life, from causing intolerable evils and thus rushing to its own destruction; it does not destroy private possessions, but safeguards them; and it does not weaken private property rights, but strengthens them. *Quadragesimo Anno,* n. 49.

On the priority of the cultural order to the economic order:

> Every country, rich or poor, has a cultural tradition handed down from past generations. This tradition includes institutions required by life in the world, and higher manifestations — artistic, intellectual and religious — of the life of the spirit. When the latter embody truly human values, it would be a great mistake to sacrifice them for the sake of the former. Any group of people who would consent to let this happen, would be giving up the better portion of their heritage; in order to live, they would be giving up their reason for living. Christ's question is directed to nations also: "What does it profit a man, if he gain the whole world but suffer the loss of his own soul?" *Populorum Progressio*, n. 40.

The economy in fact is only one aspect and one dimension of the whole of human activity. If economic life is absolutized, if the production and consumption of goods become the centre of social life and society's only value, not subject to any other value, the reason is to be found not so much in the economic system itself as in the fact that the entire socio-cultural system, by ignoring the ethical and religious dimension, has been weakened, and ends by limiting itself to the production of goods and services alone. [79]

All of this can be summed up by repeating once more that economic freedom is only one element of human freedom. When it becomes autonomous, when man is seen more as a producer or consumer of goods than as a subject who produces and consumes in order to live, then economic freedom loses its necessary relationship to the

human person and ends up by alienating and oppressing him. *Centesimus Annus,* n. 39.

Notes

[1] Duncan Hayward, "Letter to the Editor," *The Tablet*, 18th October, 1952, 15. It should be noted that Mr. Hayward, at least at the time that he made this keen observation, was a Protestant.

[2] With respect to this particular question concerning the relationship existing between Social Credit and Catholic social teaching, I am deeply indebted in all that follows to the pioneering work of Alain Pilote of the Pilgrims of Saint Michael. Cf. Alain Pilote, *The Social Credit proposals explained in 10 lessons and viewed in the light of the social doctrine of the Church* (Rougemont, Québec: The Pilgrims of Saint Michael, 2008), 113-147.

[3] The fact that there is no contradiction between the Church's social doctrine and the social philosophy behind Social Credit is a happy state of affairs which is notably absent, for example, when one considers some of the implications which the underlying 'philosophies' of Lutheranism, Calvinism, Puritanism in general, and Talmudic Judaism (above all) happen to bear with respect to Social Credit thought. This is not to suggest in the slightest that any particular group of Protestants or that Protestants in general cannot or ought not to be Social Crediters. Indeed, some of the greatest Social Crediters in history, such as the first Social Credit premier of Alberta, William Aberhart, were ardent Christians of various Protestant persuasions. These individuals overcame whatever antithetical tendencies exist within certain currents of Protestant theology and philosophy to embrace Douglas' outlook as being perfectly in line with the teaching of Christ. More broadly, let it be clear that Social Credit can be and ought to be supported by all men of good will, of any religion and of no religion, simply because it is grounded in the truth.

⁴ As was will be explained in a forthcoming publication, although Douglas did not purposefully set out to base his Social Credit ideas on the Christian worldview but rather on what showed itself in experience to be real, it nevertheless turned out that the specific worldview that he had been developing more or less independently was identical with the authentic Christian 'philosophy' or conception of reality:

"Social Credit is Christian, not primarily because it was designed to be Christian, but because it was painstakingly 'dis'-(un)-covered reality. If Christianity is not real, it is nothing; it is not 'true', it *is Truth*." C.H. Douglas, *The Development of World Dominion* (Sydney: Tidal Publications, 1969), 15.

⁵ Ibid., 49. *The Social Crediter* was and remains (now incorporated into *The Social Artist*) the official journalistic organ of the Social Credit Secretariat.

⁶ The chief aspects of socialism and communism that were objectionable according to Pope Pius XI's encyclical, *Quadragesimo Anno*, included the doctrines of materialism and the class struggle, the suppression of private property, and the domination of economic life by the state over the freedom and initiative of individuals. Douglas agreed wholeheartedly with the Church's condemnation: "It appears to be axiomatic, as the Roman Catholic Church contends, that Socialism and Communism must be fought by any church which calls itself Christian...." C.H. Douglas, *The Realistic Position of the Church of England* (Liverpool: K.R.P. Publications Ltd., 1948), 11. Unfortunately, in the contemporary Church, there are plenty of 'Catholics' who, due to their support of radical leftist economics and/or social policy, are at least material if not also formal heretics.

[7] Cf. [Commission d'étude sur le système monétaire appelé Crédit Social], "Le Crédit Social et la Doctrine Catholique", *La Semaine Religieuse de Montréal*, 15 novembre 1939 : «La Commission répond donc négativement à la question : « Le Crédit Social est-il entâché de socialisme ? » Elle ne voit pas comment on pourrait condamner au nom de l'Église et de sa doctrine sociale les principes essentiels de ce système, tels qu'exposés précédemment.»

[8] Cf. Bryan W. Monahan, *An Introduction to Social Credit*, 2nd ed. (London: K.R.P. Publications Ltd., 1967), 119.

[9] Cf. *Deus Caritas Est*, n. 29:

"We have seen that the formation of just structures is not directly the duty of the Church, but belongs to the world of politics, the sphere of the autonomous use of reason. The Church has an indirect duty here, in that she is called to contribute to the purification of reason and to the reawakening of those moral forces without which just structures are neither established nor prove effective in the long run.

The direct duty to work for a just ordering of society, on the other hand, is proper to the lay faithful. As citizens of the State, they are called to take part in public life in a personal capacity. So they cannot relinquish their participation 'in the many different economic, social, legislative, administrative and cultural areas, which are intended to promote organically and institutionally the *common good*.' [21] The mission of the lay faithful is therefore to configure social life correctly, respecting its legitimate autonomy and cooperating with other citizens according to their respective competences and fulfilling their own responsibility."

[10] Cf., for example, *Quadragesimo Anno*, n. 41: "Yet before proceeding to explain these matters, that principle which Leo XIII so clearly established must be laid down at the outset here, namely, that there resides in Us the right and duty to pronounce with supreme authority upon social and economic matters.[27] Certainly the Church was not given the commission to guide men to an only fleeting and perishable happiness but to that which is eternal. Indeed 'the Church holds that it is unlawful for her to mix without cause in these temporal concerns'[28]; however, she can in no wise renounce the duty God entrusted to her to interpose her authority, not of course in matters of technique for which she is neither suitably equipped nor endowed by office, but in all things that are connected with the moral law. For as to these, the deposit of truth that God committed to Us and the grave duty of disseminating and interpreting the whole moral law, and of urging it in season and out of season, bring under and subject to Our supreme jurisdiction not only social order but economic activities themselves."

Cf. also *Divini Redemptoris*, n. 34: "The Church does not separate a proper regard for temporal welfare from solicitude for the eternal. If she subordinates the former to the latter according to the words of her divine Founder, 'Seek ye first the Kingdom of God and His justice, and all these things shall be added unto you,'[18] she is nevertheless so far from being unconcerned with human affairs, so far from hindering civil progress and material advancement, that she actually fosters and promotes them in the most sensible and efficacious manner. Thus even in the sphere of social-economics, although the Church has never proposed a definite technical system, since this is not her field, she has nevertheless clearly outlined the guiding principles which, while susceptible of varied concrete applications according to the diversified conditions of times and places and peoples, indicate the safe way of securing the happy progress of society."

Once again, Douglas's views on this particular question are found to be in complete agreement with the Catholic position: "[N]ot only should I not object to the interest of the Church dignitaries in the matters of the everyday life of this world, but it appears to me to be axiomatic that a religion must have a politics, although not a technical politics." C.H. Douglas, *The Realistic Position of the Church of England* (Liverpool: K.R.P. Publications Ltd., 1948), 3.

[11] Cf. *Sollicitudo Rei Socialis*, n. 41: "[T]he Church does not propose economic and political systems or programs, nor does she show preference for one or the other, provided that human dignity is properly respected and promoted, and provided she herself is allowed the room she needs to exercise her ministry in the world."

[12] Cf. C.H. Douglas, *The Development of World Dominion* (Sydney: Tidal Publications, 1969), 21.

[13] In presenting the Church's social teaching I have relied heavily (though not exclusively) on the various papal encyclicals which were specifically (though not always solely) dedicated to social issues. The social encyclicals are, arguably, at least 12 in number; they are: *Vix Pervenit* (Benedict XIV – 1745), *Rerum Novarum* (Leo XIII – 1891), *Quas Primas* (Pius XI – 1925), *Quadragesimo Anno* (Pius XI – 1931), *Mater et Magistra* (John XXIII – 1961), *Pacem in Terris* (John XXIII – 1963), *Populorum Progressio* (Paul VI – 1967), *Laborem Exercens* (John Paul II – 1981), *Sollicitudo Rei Socialis* (John Paul II – 1987), *Centesimus Annus* (John Paul II – 1991), *Deus Caritas Est* (Benedict XVI – 2005), and *Caritas in Veritate* (Benedict XVI – 2009). There are other encyclicals such as *Divini Redemptoris* (Pius XI – 1937), *Redemptor Hominis* (John Paul II – 1979), and *Dives in Misericordia* (John Paul II – 1980) which touch on questions of social doctrine in the course of addressing other matters. Unfortunately, neither the aforementioned, nor the many other encyclicals which various Popes have promulgated are read as widely or as often as they should be. These letters to the universal Church from the highest ecclesial authority can all be found on-line at www.papalencyclicals.net, at the Vatican's website, and in a variety of other locations.

[14] The *Compendium of the Social Doctrine of the Church* is an authoritative document which was released by the Pontifical Council for Justice and Peace in 2004. It draws heavily on Sacred Revelation and on the authoritative interpretation of that revelation which has been provided by the social encyclicals of various Popes.

It might be objected that the Church's social teaching ought to be summarily rejected because the institutional church or certain layers within it have sometimes operated in a manner which is at odds with the very principles it champions. This objection commits the *tu quoque* fallacy. While it is true that the institutional church has indeed failed, at various levels, at various times, and in various places, to live up to its own teaching, this does not entitle one to conclude that the teaching is therefore false. The discrepancy existing between theory and practice is better interpreted as a call for Catholics to effectively demand that the clerical and other administrative hierarchies of the institutional church operate, at all times, in full conformity with the social doctrine of the Church.

The Church has a highly developed social doctrine because she recognizes, *inter alia*, that there is an intimate connection between man's temporal and eternal welfare. Very often the adequate fulfillment of the former is, practically speaking, a necessary or at least a positive inductive condition for the realization of the latter:

"Yet it is not rash by any means to say that the whole scheme of social and economic life is now such as to put in the way of vast numbers of mankind most serious obstacles which prevent them from caring for the one thing necessary; namely, their eternal salvation."*Quadragesimo Anno*, n. 130.

Apart from this overarching concern, the social doctrine of the Church is also a necessary part of her teaching because the moral law, obedience to which is necessary for salvation, requires that associations operate in keeping with the correct ethical principles, i.e., those principles under which associations function best. Catholics therefore have a serious moral duty to work for the re-ordering of all associations of which they are a part in light of those principles.

Far from ignoring or denigrating the things of this world in view of a future state of existence, authentic Christianity teaches that the things of this world must also be transformed and be brought into alignment with the source and destiny of all created things, i.e., God. The seed of the beatific vision must be planted and begin its transformational development of the created order here below:

"on the one hand, religion must not be restricted 'to the purely private sphere' [96]; on the other, the Christian message must not be relegated to a purely other-worldly salvation incapable of shedding light on our earthly existence [97].

Because of the public relevance of the Gospel and faith, because of the corrupting effects of injustice, that is, of sin, the Church cannot remain indifferent to social matters [98]. 'To the Church belongs the right always and everywhere to announce moral principles, including those pertaining to the social order, and to make judgements on any human affairs to the extent that they are required by the fundamental rights of the human person or the salvation of souls.' [99]." *Compendium of the Social Doctrine of the Church*, n. 71.

[15] Cf. Ibid., n. 106: "*All of social life is an expression of its unmistakable protagonist: the human person*. The Church has many times and in many ways been the authoritative advocate of this understanding, recognizing and affirming the centrality of the human person in every sector and expression of society: 'Human society is therefore the object of the social teaching of the Church since she is neither outside nor over and above socially united men, but exists exclusively in them and, therefore, for them'[200]. This important awareness is expressed in the affirmation that 'far from being the object or passive element of social life' the human person 'is rather, and must always remain, its subject, foundation and goal'[201]. The origin of social life is therefore found in the human person, and society cannot refuse to recognize its active and responsible subject; every expression of society must be directed towards the human person."

Cf. also, *Guadium et Spes*, n. 26: "[T]here is a growing awareness of the exalted dignity proper to the human person, since he stands above all things, and his rights and duties are universal and inviolable. ... Hence, the social order and its development must invariably work to the benefit of the human person if the disposition of affairs is to be subordinate to the personal realm and not contrariwise, as the Lord indicated when He said that the Sabbath was made for man, and not man for the Sabbath.(6)"

Cf. also, *Compendium of the Social Doctrine of the Church*, n. 132. "Respect for human dignity can in no way be separated from obedience to this principle. It is necessary to 'consider every neighbour without exception as another self, taking into account first of all his life and the means necessary for living it with dignity.' Every political, economic, social, scientific and cultural program must be inspired by the awareness of the primacy of each human being over society."[248]

[16] C.H. Douglas, *Economic Democracy*, 5th ed. (Sudbury: Bloomfield Publishers, 1974), 29.

[17] *Gaudium et Spes*, n. 26.

[18] *Populorum Progressio*, n. 14.

[19] C.H. Douglas, *Economic Democracy*, 5th ed. (Sudbury, England: Bloomfield Books, 1974), 142-143.

[20] Cf. C.H. Douglas, *The Development of World Dominion* (Sydney: Tidal Publications, 1969), 43.

[21] Cf. *Compendium of the Social Doctrine of the Church*, n.187: "This principle [of subsidiarity - OH] is imperative because every person, family and intermediate group has something original to offer to the community. Experience shows that the denial of subsidiarity, or its limitation in the name of an alleged democratization or equality of all members of society, limits and sometimes even destroys the spirit of freedom and initiative.

The principle of subsidiarity is opposed to certain forms of centralization, bureaucratization, and welfare assistance, and to the unjustified and excessive presence of the State in public mechanisms."

[22] C.H. Douglas, *Economic Democracy*, 5th ed. (Sudbury, England: Bloomfield Books, 1974), 30.

[23] Cf. *Quadragesimo Anno*, n. 71: "It is an intolerable abuse, and to be abolished at all cost, for mothers on account of the father's low wage to be forced to engage in gainful occupations outside of the home to the neglect of their proper cares and duties, especially the training of children."

[24] Cf. Ibid., 114: "For certain kinds of property, it is rightly contended, ought to be reserved to the State since they carry with them a dominating power so great that cannot without danger to the general welfare be entrusted to private individuals."

[25] When they are both correctly understood there can be no question, therefore, of subsidiarity being promoted at the expense of solidarity or vice-versa. The two principles are mutually dependent and mutually supporting when they are interpreted as a mere means for achieving the common good rather than as possessing any kind of static validity as ends in themselves.

[26] C.H. Douglas, *Economic Democracy*, 5th ed. (Sudbury, England: Bloomfield Books), 28. In the same spirit, Douglas once counseled against "an exaggerated individualism, far removed from genuine individuality." C.H. Douglas, *Warning Democracy*, 3rd ed. (London: Stanley Nott, 1935), 118.

[27] Cf. *Sollicitudo Rei Socialis*, n. 30: "Anyone wishing to renounce the difficult yet noble task of improving the lot of man in his totality, and of all people, with the excuse that the struggle is difficult and that constant effort is required, or simply because of the experience of defeat and the need to begin again, that person would be betraying the will of God the Creator." Cf. also, ibid., n. 38: "This determination is based on the solid conviction that what is hindering full development is that desire for profit and that thirst for power already mentioned. These attitudes and 'structures of sin' are only conquered – presupposing the help of divine grace – by a diametrically opposed attitude: a commitment to the good of one's neighbour with the readiness, in the gospel sense, to 'lose oneself' for the sake of the other instead of exploiting him, and to 'serve him' instead of oppressing him for one's own advantage...."

[28] C.H. Douglas, *The Approach to Reality* (London: K.R.P. Publications Ltd., 1936), 5.

[29] Father Peter Coffey, who held a doctorate in Philosophy and was a professor at Maynooth College in Ireland, had contributed to Douglas' quarterly *The Fig Tree*. It is reported that in March of 1932 he had written the following to a Canadian Jesuit, Father Richard:

"The difficulties raised by your questions can be met only by the reform of the financial system of capitalism along the lines suggested by Major Douglas and the Social Credit school of credit reform. It is the accepted financing system that is at the root of the evils of capitalism. The accuracy of the analysis carried out by Douglas has never been refuted. I believe that, with their famous price-regulation formula, the Douglas reform proposals are the only reform that will go to the root of the evil...." Cf. Alain Pilote, *The Social Credit proposals explained in 10 lessons and viewed in the light of the social doctrine of the Church* (Rougemont, Québec: The Pilgrims of Saint Michael, 2008), 141.

[30] Cf. for example, Maritain's last text, entitled: "A Society without Money", which was completed on the night before his death on April 29, 1973. Jacques Maritain, "A Society without Money", *Review of Social Economy* Vol. 43, No. 1 (April, 1985): 73-83.

[31] Cf. John Finlay, *Social Credit: the English Origins* (Montréal and London: McGill-Queen's University Press, 1972), 217-233.

[32] Cf. Alain Pilote, *The Social Credit proposals explained in 10 lessons.* (Rougemont, Québec: The Pilgrims of Saint Michael, 2008), 145.

[33]

http://www.vatican.va/holy_father/john_paul_ii/speeches/1984/september/documents/hf_jp-ii_spe_19840912_pescatori-terranova_en.html.

[35] http://www.papalencyclicals.net/Ben14/b14vixpe.htm. The encyclical *Vix Pervenit* was promulgated on the 1st of November, 1745 by Pope Benedict XIV. After having consulted at great length with various cardinals, theologians, and canon lawyers, the Pope presented their findings with the aim of establishing a 'fixed teaching on usury'. The encyclical, in keeping with statements made by previous ecumenical councils, earlier Popes, and indeed the whole Christian tradition, condemned the charging of interest when it is understood as an intrinsic right which is supposedly grounded in the very act of lending money. The idea is that the act of loaning money to someone does not, by itself, justly entitle the lender to receive an additional amount of money over and above the sum which he had originally lent. Any profit made in this way is considered illegitimate because it introduces inequality into the exchange.

The maintenance of harmonious, interdependent relations requires that the exchanges which lie at the heart of economic life observe what has been called the principle of capitalist justice: they ought to be equally mutually beneficial. If someone who grows carrots, for example, wishes to exchange a pound of carrots for a pound of lettuce grown by his neighbour, both parties to the transaction benefit in a quantitatively equal way by obtaining something which is more valuable to them than that which they gave up in the exchange. One wouldn't, however, accept a pound of carrots from another carrot farmer in exchange for two pounds of carrots because, in this case, only one party to the transaction would derive any benefit at all (the first carrot farmer would have an even greater surplus to sell *ex hypothesi* to the lettuce grower, while the second would have less of a surplus). And yet, when it comes to money, lending a sum of money and expecting in return, simply on account of the loan, that same sum plus an additional amount leads precisely to the same type of asymmetrical exchange (although in this case the borrower does derive some benefit by temporarily gaining access to money he did not have before). The lender is in fact charging for the use of the money itself when money is (or ought to be) nothing more than a simple instrument which has been introduced to facilitate economic exchanges, or, more broadly, the cycles of production and consumption. In this connection it should be noted that the norms of commutative justice require that ill-gotten gains must be returned to the disadvantaged party in restitution.

Now, the encyclical does recognize that there can indeed be extrinsic titles or justifications for the lender's demand for more money than he had lent, although it does not specify what those would be. Catholic theologians and Church authorities have considered a number of possibilities. Take, for example, the case where someone's loan were to assist in the financing of a productive enterprise. In this situation the lender could justly regard it as a temporary investment on the basis of which a share in the profits (or a dividend) could and should be distributed (provided that there are profits). Extrinsic justifications could also be invoked whenever the lender could honestly claim compensation for the risk, the losses due to inflation, the opportunity costs, and/or the delays involved in lending. As we have seen, receiving more money in return for money lent is usurious, immoral, and should be prohibited *in the absence of any legitimate extrinsic title*, but even in this case the volume of additional money demanded must not be excessive if the norms of capitalist justice are to be duly respected *and* the borrower must have an easy and legitimate way of obtaining the difference; i.e., overall prices and available purchasing power must be kept in balance by the financial system. Since, under the current system, no attempt is made to compensate for the inherent sterility of money, i.e., the fact that lending money cannot by itself breed more money with which the interest charge might be paid (as many philosophers such as Aristotle, St. Thomas Aquinas, and Jacques Maritain have noted), it is doubtful whether, as a matter of fact (as opposed to principle), any and all extrinsic justifications could be sufficient, under existing conditions, to restore equality to monetary exchanges.

In any case, the reader will duly note that, as it has been defined by the Church, usury is not the charging of interest on a loan or the reception of a larger quantity of money in exchange for a loan as such, but rather the charging of interest on a monetary exchange under conditions which make the exchange intrinsically unequal or exploitative.

In the opinion of the present author, it would seem that demanding substantial interest payments on the basis of lending money which is created by a fraudulent and monopolistic banking system *ex nihilo*, and at very little cost to its creators, does indeed qualify as the sort of unequal monetary exchange which the encyclical condemns. Unfortunately, in the past few centuries, the institutional church (probably on account of its own compromises with and dependence on contemporary finance) has consistently failed to actively promulgate and enforce the Church's social doctrine as it applies to financial questions. As a matter of fact, this particular encyclical, which may rightly be regarded as the very first of the Church's social encyclicals, remains largely unknown in Catholic circles, and, in the pre-internet era, copies of it were quite difficult to obtain.

[35]

http://www.vatican.va/holy_father/john_paul_ii/speeches/1984/september/documents/hf_jp-ii_spe_19840912_pescatori-terranova_en.html.

[36]

http://www.vatican.va/holy_father/john_paul_ii/speeches/1980/july/documents/hf_jp-ii_spe_19800703_operai-brasile_po.html

"Uma condição essencial é a de der [sic] à economia um sentido e uma lógica humanas [sic]. Vale aqui o que eu disse a respeito do trabalho. É preciso libertar os diversos campos da existência do domínio de um economismo avassalador. É preciso pôr as exigências económicas no seu devido lugar e criar um tecido social multiforme, que impeça a massificação. Ninguém está dispensado de colaborar nessa tarefa. ... Cristãos, em qualquer lugar onde estiverem, assumam a sua parte de responsabilidade neste imenso esforço pela reestruturação inumana [sic] da cidade. A fé fez disto um dever."

[37]

http://www.vatican.va/holy_father/john_paul_ii/letters/1985/documents/hf_jp-ii_let_19850926_mons-mcintyre_fr.html.

« Je tiens encore à aborder une question délicate et douloureuse. Je veux parler du tourment des responsables de plusieurs pays, qui ne savent plus comment faire face à l'angoissant problème de l'endettement. Sans vouloir entrer dans des considérations techniques, je désire cependant mentionner ce problème qui constitue un des aspects les plus complexes de la situation générale de l'économie internationale. Une réforme structurelle du système financier mondial est sans nul doute une des initiatives qui apparaissent les plus urgentes et nécessaires. »

Bibliography

Benedict XIV. *Vix Pervenit*, 1745.
Benedict XVI. *Caritas in Veritate*, 2009.
—. *Deus Caritas Est*, 2005.
Catechism of the Catholic Church, second edition. Libreria Editrice Vaticana, 1994.
[Commission d'étude sur le système monétaire appelé Crédit social]. "Le Crédit Social et la Doctrine Catholique." *La Semaine Religieuse de Montréal*, 15 novembre, 1939 : n/a
Compendium of the Social Doctrine of the Church. Libreria Editrice Vaticana, 2004
Dobbs, Geoffrey. *What is Social Credit?* Sudbury, England: Bloomfield Books, 1981.
Douglas, C.H. *The Approach to Reality*. London: K.R.P. Publications Ltd., 1936.
—. *The Development of World Dominion*. Sydney: Tidal Publications, 1969.
—. *Economic Democracy*. 5th ed. Sudbury, England: Bloomfield Books, 1974.
—. *The Realistic Position of the Church of England*. K.R.P. Publications Ltd., 1948.
—. *Warning Democracy*. 3rd ed. London: Stanley Nott, 1935.
Even, Louis. *In this Age of Plenty*. Rougemont, Québec: The Pilgrims of Saint Michael, 1996.
—. *Une Lumière Sur Mon Chemin*. Rougemont, Québec: Les Pèlerins de Saint Michel, 2010.
—. *What do We Mean by Real Social Credit? Above Political Parties*. Rougemont, Québec: The Pilgrims of Saint Michael, 1990.
Finlay, John. *Social Credit: the English Origins*. Montréal and London: McGill-Queen's University Press, 1972.

Hayward, Duncan. "Letter to the Editor." *The Tablet*, 18th, October, 1952, 15.

Heydorn, M. Oliver. *Social Credit Economics*. Ancaster, Ontario: CreateSpace, 2014.

John XXIII. *Mater et Magistra*, 1961.

—. *Pacem in Terris*, 1963.

John Paul II. *Centesimus Annus*, 1991.

—. *Dives in Misercordia*, 1980.

—. *Laborem Exercens*, 1981.

—. *Redemptor Hominis*, 1979.

—. *Sollicitudo Rei Socialis*, 1987.

Leo XIII. *Rerum Novarum*, 1891.

Levesque, George-Henri. *Social Credit and Catholicism*. http://www.alor.org/Library/Social%20Credit%20and%20Catholicism.htm

Maritain, Jacques. "A Society Without Money." *Review of Social Economy* Vol. 43, No. 1 (April, 1985): 73-83.

Monahan, Bryan W. *An Introduction to Social Credit*, 2nd ed. London: K.R.P. Publications Ltd., 1967.

Paul VI. *Populorum Progressio*, 1967.

Pilote, Alain. *La démocratie économique expliquée en 10 leçons: et vue à la lumière de la doctrine sociale de l'église.* Rougemont, Québec: Les Pèlerins de Saint-Michel, 2009.

—. *The Social Credit proposals explained in 10 lessons and viewed in the light of the social doctrine of the Church*. Rougemont, Québec: The Pilgrims of Saint Michael, 2008.

Pius XI. *Divini Redemptoris*, 1937.

—.*Quadragesimo Anno*, 1931.

Vatican Council II. "*Gaudium et Spes* [Pastoral Constitution on the Church in the Modern World]." In *The Vatican Collection: The Conciliar and Postconciliar Documents*, vol. 1, edited by Austin Flannery, 903-1001. Northport, NY: Costello, 1996.

Made in the USA
Lexington, KY
29 November 2017